AGAINST THE NIGHT

STUDY GUIDE

AGAINST THE NIGHT

CHARLES COLSON

STUDY GUIDE
By Art Lindsley

VINE
BOOKS

Servant Publications
Ann Arbor, Michigan

Grateful acknowledgment is made for the editorial contributions of Ellen Santilli Vaughn and Camilla Luckey.

Cover design by Michael Andaloro
Cover Photo from Four by Five

Vine books is an imprint of Servant Publications especially designed to serve Evangelical Christians.

Published by Servant Publications
P.O. Box 8617
Ann Arbor, Michigan 48107

Printed in the United States of America
ISBN 0-89283-652-0

89 90 91 92 93 10 9 8 7 6 5 4 3 2 1

CONTENTS

INTRODUCTION

This companion study guide for Charles Colson's book, *Against the Night*, is designed to help the reader interact with the issues and ideas the book raises. *Against the Night* conveys significant material helping us to understand the state of our culture and how to respond to it. The studies in this volume will help you understand the context of the book; each chapter of the study guide focuses on a theme from *Against the Night*, highlighting first the issue or idea in general and then how it applies to everyday life.

It is important to recognize that the intention of this study is not the furthering of knowledge alone. Rather, our purpose here is to facilitate action—putting learning into practice. Thus equipped, Christians can make a significant difference in the communities and cultural context of which they are a part.

Personal Study

As you read *Against the Night* and reflect on the issues the book raises, this guide will serve as a catalyst for continued reflection and personal application.

As you use this guide, set aside time, a copy of *Against the Night*, a Bible, a notebook, and a pen. Be sure to read the sections from *Against the Night* and the Bible that are indicated at the beginning of each study chapter.

If you have any questions about any of the issues or

questions raised in this study, be sure to discuss them with your pastor or a leader in your church.

Group Study

This study is also well suited for group study. Divided into 13 chapters, it fits into a Sunday school quarter, or into a weekly Bible study or home group.

Preparation is essential for a group study. Before coming together for discussion, everyone in the group should read the appropriate Scripture passages and book chapters so the group can delve into discussion.

Leaders for group studies should read at least one week ahead in both the book and the study guide in order to add discussion topics that will make each study specifically applicable. In the studies on the family, education, and politics, for example, leaders might consider inviting a guest speaker to address the group. Or, individuals could read some of the books suggested for further study and then report back to the rest of the group. Think creatively about how to use the book and adapt its teachings to the specific needs of your group.

Study Scripture

Each of the 13 study chapters follow the same format. The framework provides a structure for organization, but should be adapted and used to fit the character of your particular group. The eight-part study format includes:

1. Introduction: A few sentences sketching the study topic.

2. Read: Designated chapters of *Against the Night* and corresponding portions of Scripture.

3. Study: Questions concerning factual material from *Against the Night* and the Scripture readings.

4. Reflect: Questions designed for personal reflection on the content's relevance to readers' lives. Responses are not necessarily right or wrong, but an opportunity to think about how God would have you apply the ideas and issues which the book examines.

5. Summarize: This section allows space for each reader to capsulize the most important lesson learned from the study.

6. Apply: This follow-up section encourages the reader to specifically apply the lessons learned, to state when and how you plan to act in the arena of your everyday life. Also, as you go through each of the studies, take time to check back to previous application sections to monitor your progress.

7. Pray: Each study ends with prayer, focusing on the topics and themes of the chapter at hand. You will then want to go on to praise, thanksgiving, confession, and intercession for particular concerns of your group.

Make sure to save sufficient time for prayer. It is through prayer that God will transform head knowledge into heart action.

8. Further Study: Suggested readings are provided for those interested in pursuing particular topics. The lists are by no means exhaustive, but provide several suggestions for additional study.

Decay and Change

Change is inevitable. Cars rust. Kids grow up. Paint peels. Hair grays. Seasons change, so do seashores, and great institutions can sometimes crumble. Some changes are unalterable, others can be hidden, and the direction of a few can be reversed.

A shadow creeps across our land. It signals the decline of our culture—the "new dark ages," the "spiritual exhaustion" of the West. But those who believe in Christ can resist this growing darkness.

No one—except our sovereign God—knows whether we face the end of the West, whether the cultural decay around us is fatal. But one thing is for sure: we have been invaded by an army of new barbarians who, without even knowing it, are advancing that decline, day by day.

READ

Against the Night: Prologue and chapter 1
Psalm 90

STUDY

1. As he watched Carthage burn, Scipio, the Roman conqueror, wept. (See page 16.) What caused him to weep, even though he had won?

2. Some changes appear inevitable that are not. And vice-versa. What changes are inevitable? What changes are not? How do these appearances fool us?

3. For Solzhenitsyn to warn the West of its "spiritual exhaustion," he had to see symptoms that we ourselves may have overlooked or ignored. What might some of those symptoms be?

4. Our state of moral decay has qualified our day to wear the label "Dark Ages." What are some of the characteristics of today's "new barbarians"? What dangers do they pose? And in what disguises can they be found?

5. Psalm 90 offers hope in a world of change, decay, and sin. What is the foundation of our hope?

REFLECT

1. Name a few inevitable changes from your own experience. Did you handle them as did the author of Psalm 90?

2. What changes in your life can be reversed?

3. All of us fall, to some extent, under the influence of the "new barbarians." What should be our attitude toward them?

SUMMARIZE

What is the most significant lesson you learned in this study?

APPLY

Could you in any way be mistaken for a "new barbarian"? If so, what would you change about yourself? How will you deal with "barbarians" who have invaded your community?

PRAY

Pray for our society, using the prayer in Psalm 90 as a starting point. Pray that God might show you what you can do.

FURTHER STUDY

Henry Fairlie, *Seven Deadly Sins Today*, University of Notre Dame, 1979.

Paul Johnson, *Modern Times*, Harper & Row, 1983.

Paul Kennedy, *The Rise and Fall of Great Powers*, Random House, 1987.

Christopher Lasch, *Culture of Narcissism*, Warner Books, 1979.

Alexander Solzhenitsyn, *Gulag Archipelago II*, Harper & Row, 1974.

Individualism

Seeds planted during the Enlightenment have rooted deep, changing our public ethic today. They include ideas that man (rather than God) is the fixed point around which everything else revolves, and that morality can be established not according to God's standards, nor even classical Aristotelian ideas of virtue, but within the mind and heart of man.

With little exception, our society is no longer guided by virtue or tradition, but by selfish passion. Truth is now pliable and relative; it can take whatever shape we want. Indeed, why not just look inside yourself to find it? Such is the nature of individualism, which can sap the lifeblood of a nation.

READ

Against the Night, chapters 2 and 3
Mark 8:34–37
1 Corinthians 13:4–7
John 8:31–32
Romans 12:3

STUDY

1. What are some examples given of the "moral pride" of individualism? (See pages 27–30.)

2. How does individualism destroy commitment? (See pages 31–33.)

3. There's a world of difference between "valuing the individual" and "individualism." Compare the two.

4. How does individualism affect families, neighborhoods, churches, and civic groups?

5. Subtly and not so subtly, the media contributes to individualism. Name some examples.

6. How does the spirit of individualism contradict what Jesus taught in Mark 8:34–37?

7. Compare an attitude of individualism with Paul's definition of love in 1 Corinthians 13:4–7.

REFLECT

1. What evidences of individualism do you see in your community?

2. We've all been influenced by individualism to some extent. What factors make it difficult at times for you to make and sustain commitments?

3. How has individualism affected your church? Your family? Yourself?

SUMMARIZE

What is the most significant lesson you learned in this study?

APPLY

How will you deal with those places around you that have been overtaken by individualism?

PRAY

Pray that God will help you resist the influence of individualism and enable you to make significant commitments to others.

FURTHER STUDY

Robert Bellah, *Habits of the Heart*, Harper & Row, 1986.
Anthony Hoekema, *The Christian Looks at Himself*, Eerdmans, 1975.
Paul Vitz, *Psychology as Religion*, Eerdmanns, 1977.
"Empowering the Self: A Look at the Human Potential Movement," *SCP Journal*, Winter 1981–82 (P.O. Box 2418, Berkeley, CA 94702).

Relativism

Jean-Paul Sartre once wrote that "no finite point has meaning without an infinite reference point." He saw, quite correctly, that unless there is a God who reveals himself and so establishes meaning, no meaning exists. Manmade meaning is nothing more than transient personal experience or volatile personal preference.

No wonder Sartre, an atheistic existentialist, despaired! Based on his assumptions, his life had no meaning. All human existence, in fact, would be meaningless.

Christians, however, need not despair. For a Christian, God—transcendent, infinite, and beyond all "personal preference"—provides the reference point. Absolute truth and values hold—in spite of relativism's assertions that truth is whatever each individual deems it to be.

READ

Against the Night, chapter 4
2 Corinthians 10:3–5
Hosea 4:6
Isaiah 59:14

STUDY

1. Before relativism overran traditional values, what were the West's foundations for "moral wisdom"? Where did our society find its standards for right and wrong? (See page 44.)

2. Since relativism, or the substitution of man's standards for objective, transcendent values, has become widely accepted, what changes can you see in our schools, media, churches, government, and other social structures? How does relativism undermine public virtue? (See pages 48–49.)

3. Relativism and individualism go hand-in-hand. Describe their relationship and how relativism undermines individual character. (See page 49.)

4. According to 2 Corinthians 10:3–5, what is our task?

5. Read Hosea 4:6 and describe what happens when God's people ignore God's thoughts.

6. Isaiah wrote about problems like those we experience today; his people turned from God. And what happened to justice, righteousness, and truth? (See Isaiah 59:14–15.)

REFLECT

1. Beliefs as firm as bedrock since early Christianity have been eroded by relativism. What eroded beliefs are more obvious? Which ones are more subtle?

2. Sometimes it's difficult to defend unpopular views or opinions. As a Christian, what values do you find hard to talk about with unbelievers? At what point does the discussion become difficult? Why? Is it ever because you yourself are unclear about your values or are affected by relativistic tendencies?

3. What values might you be tempted to compromise at work or in the community, or even in your home?

4. How can we discern and decide what's right among the competing values in our culture?

5. How can we know which claims of authority to trust?

SUMMARIZE

What is the most significant lesson you learned in this study?

APPLY

Can you identify places eroded by relativism, even relativistic choices you have made? How will you strengthen those areas?

PRAY

Pray that God helps you grasp and maintain his truth in a day of shifting values.

FURTHER STUDY

Allan Bloom, *The Closing of the American Mind*, Simon & Schuster, 1987.
Francis Schaeffer, *The God Who Is There*, InterVarsity, 1968.
Francis Schaeffer, *How Should We Then Live?*, Crossway, 1983.

Loss of Character

We should not be surprised at the crisis of character we see around us.

Our character is rooted in what we think. It has been said: "Sow a thought, reap an act: sow an act, reap a habit; sow a habit, reap a character; sow a character, reap a destiny." Or we could say, "For want of a thought, an act is lost; for want of an act, a habit is lost; for want of a habit, a character is lost; for want of a character, a destiny is lost."

Swapping honor for pleasure, a popular trade, turns out to be a bad deal. Hedonism, the race to attain pleasure and avoid pain, can be a never-ending—and empty—pursuit.

READ

Against the Night, chapters 5 and 6
Romans 5:3–5
Colossians 3:12–17
Romans 12:2

STUDY

1. What is social critic Russell Kirk's definition of decadence? (See page 56.)

2. We associate various virtues—courage, compassion, duty—with character; we rely on these individual virtues to maintain the common good. What happens to society when these virtues disappear?

3. What did C. S. Lewis mean by his phrase, "men without chests"? (See pages 66–67.)

4. Why did the story of Clayton Lonetree, the young Marine guard at the American embassy in Moscow who traded national secrets for sex and cash, so catch the public's imagination?

5. Not only individuals lose their character and conscience. How have public institutions been affected by the loss of character? (See pages 68–69.)

6. Certain qualities are to be found in those who believe in Christ. How does the list of virtues (kindness, patience, gentleness, and so forth) in Colossians 3:12–17 compare to the crisis of character in our culture at large?

7. How can trials build character? (See Romans 5:3–5.)

8. What does Romans 12:2 say about transforming our character? What connection does this Scripture make between character and thought?

REFLECT

1. What examples of loss of character have you noticed in your experience?

2. What does it take to reverse the direction of character in someone's life?

3. What makes it so hard to break bad habits and establish good ones?

4. How has the church been affected by the culture's loss of character?

SUMMARIZE

What is the most significant lesson you learned in this study?

APPLY

How can you guard your own character and help others guard theirs?

PRAY

Pray that God will help you grow in character and encourage others in the same direction. Pray that the direction of culture will be reversed.

FURTHER STUDY

Dietrich Bonhoeffer, *The Cost of Discipleship*, Macmillan, 1963.

Stanley Hauerwas, *Character and the Christian Life*, Trinity University Press, 1985.

Stanley Hauerwas, *A Community of Character*, Notre Dame Press, 1981.

C.S. Lewis, *Abolition of Man*, Macmillan, 1978.

The Family

One of the most evident crises of our time is the break-up of marriages and families. G.K. Chesterton maintained that many people say they want divorce "without ever asking themselves whether they want marriage." Perhaps they never gave serious thought to the fact that marriage and family are actually the most basic unit of human organization and civilization, the first school of human instruction. Not only does family break-up leave children vulnerable to all sorts of emotional harm, it leaves them uneducated in lessons of conscience and character. The result is moral illiteracy.

Putting biblical principles back into marriage and family, and marriage and family back into place as the cornerstone in our society's foundations, is key to rebuilding in our society those qualities of character vital to survival.

READ

Against the Night, chapter 7
Matthew 19:1–12

Ephesians 5:22–6:4
Colossians 3:18–21

STUDY

1. The break-up of the traditional family has public and private consequences. Name several.

2. Why is there a relationship between crime and the failure of the family? (See page 73.)

3. Who is to blame for America's family meltdown? (See page 75–76.)

4. According to Robert Bellah, individualists consider contracts valid only if "commitments" are in their own best interests; if contracts fail to meet their needs, they break them. How can this point of view destroy family life? Society?

5. What part should the family play in children's moral education?

6. In Matthew 19:1–12, how did Jesus define God's intention for marriage?

7. Based upon Ephesians 5:22–33, how are husbands and wives to treat each other? When they don't, what is the harm to the family?

8. How are parents to treat children, based upon Ephesians 6:1–4 and Colossians 3:18–21?

REFLECT

1. Scarcely any family remains untouched by divorce. Keeping in mind the lack of moral influence in most marriages, give some central reasons for the divorces you have observed.

2. What responsibility do we have to confront friends' noticeable marital problems before it's too late?

3. What are the difficulties in being a single parent? How can friends give support?

4. If parents don't "civilize" their children, who does? What are the dangers of leaving childhood training to amoral or immoral caretakers?

5. What are some specific ideas to strengthen families?

SUMMARIZE

What is the most significant lesson you learned in this study?

APPLY

How can you better model moral virtue, strengthening not just your own family, but those that look to you?

PRAY

Pray that God will help you be faithful in your family situation. Pray that there might be a widespread recovery of family values in our nation.

FURTHER STUDY

James Dobson, *Dare to Discipline*, Tyndale, 1977.
James Dobson, *Love for a Lifetime*, Multnomah, 1987.
Edith Schaeffer, *What Is a Family?*, Revell, 1982.
Gary Smalley, *The Blessing*, Nelson, 1986.

Education

"There is one thing a professor can be absolutely certain of: almost every student entering the university believes, or says he believes, that truth is relative." Thus begins Allan Bloom's best-selling book, *The Closing of the American Mind.* "Openness" is the only virtue, says Bloom, that education today inculcates.

Relativism quenches the thirst for truth, so that the quest for it ends before it ever properly begins. To find that one perspective is superior to another (or, even worse; to discover a dividing line between good and evil) would betray the current commitment of liberal education to openness. So, ironically, what is taught as "openness" is actually "closedness"—the closing of the American mind to the possibility of truth and the necessity of pursuing it.

READ

Against the Night, chapter 8
Proverbs 9:8–9
Proverbs 15:31

Proverbs 21:11
Proverbs 25:12

STUDY

1. What is the real crisis of American education? Barbara Walters described the new generation of students as "undisciplined cultural barbarians." What characteristics of today's high-schoolers led her to this conclusion? (See pages 79–80.)

2. So-called "value neutral education" claims to teach no values, but in fact, does promote a value system. Describe the smorgasbord system of morally-equivalent life-styles it promotes—and how that system runs counter to the moral restraints essential to character. (See pages 81–82.)

3. What is the "new tolerance" or openness that Allan Bloom describes? (See page 84.) Give some examples of how that openness can affect curricula.

4. Compare what Plato gave as the goal for education to what actually happens in today's campuses.

5. In the Proverbs passages given at the beginning of this study, what is the wise person open to?

REFLECT

1. Name some good and bad kinds of openness.

2. We need to maintain tolerance, in its good sense, in several forms: legal, social, intellectual. How can we have tolerance without letting it slip into relativism?

3. Can you think of examples of good and bad kinds of closedness?

4. Propose some solutions to our educational problems.

SUMMARIZE

What is the most significant lesson you learned in this study?

APPLY

What can you do to make sure any students within your influence are headed in the direction of truth?

PRAY

Pray that you may be open to God's truth and open to reproof. Pray for God's wisdom. Pray that you might be closed to compromising God's truth.

FURTHER READING

Allan Bloom, *The Closing of the American Mind*, Simon & Schuster, 1987.

C.S. Lewis, *The Abolition of Man*, Macmillan, 1978.

Alasdair MacIntyre, *After Virtue*, 2d ed., Notre Dame Press, 1984.

Politics

Pick up any newspaper and you see why "ethics in politics" sounds like a contradiction in terms. Disillusionment is widespread. Watergate, the Iran-Contra affair, indictments everywhere and accusations of ethical violations against politicians: all raise the question of character in national government. So do the cases of corruption that abound on the state and local levels. According to a recent survey comparing perceptions of the ethical integrity of various professions, people in government are almost at the bottom. Government, as every other institution of our society, shows the impact of relativism and individualism.

READ

Against the Night, chapter 9
Romans 13:1–7
2 Chronicles 7:14

STUDY

1. What are some of the examples given of the loss of character in government? (See pages 89–92.)

2. What is pluralism traditionally? (See pages 92–93.)

3. What is the "new pluralism"? (See page 93.)

4. What is the impact of the loss of transcendent standards on government? (See page 93.)

5. What is the role of the "common good" in thinking about the nation?

6. What is the source of government power (authority) in Romans 13:1–7?

7. What is government's role with respect to good and evil in Romans 13?

8. What are the conditions and promises in 2 Chronicles 7:14?

REFLECT

1. What role should faith play in the making of laws?

2. Why does "separation of church and state" not mean the separation of the state from God?

3. Does pluralism necessarily lead to relativism? Suggest some ways we could return from the "new pluralism" (with its lack of transcendent standards) to the old.

4. What can we expect government to do for society?

5. In order to recover a view of "public service" or a vision for the "common good," we need to make some changes. Describe them.

6. Some say politics should never be based on self-interest. Do you agree? Substantiate your answer.

SUMMARIZE

What is the most significant lesson you learned in this study?

APPLY

How have you, perhaps through economic interests or causes you support, contributed to the condition of our government? How can you use your influence to help your leaders and legislators restore transcendent values to the decision-making process?

PRAY

Pray that we might humble ourselves, seek God's face, repent of our sins, and God will hear from heaven and forgive our sin and heal our land.

FURTHER STUDY

Charles Colson, *Kingdoms in Conflict*, Morrow/Zondervan, 1987.

Richard Neuhaus, *The Naked Public Square*, Eerdmans, 1984.

Richard Neuhaus and M. Cromartie, *Piety and Politics*, Ethics & Public Policy Center, 1987.

The Church

Although religion is on the rise in America, morality is not. As George Gallup put it, "religion up, morality down." That paradox could be explained by the fact that the beliefs that pass for religion in most churches appear to be manmade. As a church, we're satisfied with mediocrity, self-indulgence, and watered-down standards. C. S. Lewis wrote in the *Weight of Glory:*

> Our Lord finds our desires not too strong but too weak. We are half-hearted creatures fooling about with drink and sex and ambition when infinite joy is offered us, like an ignorant child who wants to go on making mud pies in a slum because he cannot imagine what is meant by the offer of a holiday at the sea. We are far too easily pleased.

Many today are far too easily pleased with what is offered by health-and-wealth preachers, "feel-good" teachers, and self-oriented new cults. Imagine how God views what goes on in the American church today, with its glitzy televangelists, bishops who bless homosexual unions, and

pew upon pew of us who hardly dare emerge from our
fellowship suppers to minister to a hurting world.

READ

Against the Night, chapters 10 and 11
1 Peter 2:9–10
Matthew 16:18

STUDY

1. No question there's a loss of morality in the church, and
not always in blatant form like homosexual marriages and
marital infidelity. Name some of the subtler forms you've
observed. How does immorality in the church make itself
at home?

2. How does televangelism contribute to the church's crip-
pled character? (See pages 102–103.)

3. To what would you attribute the New Age movement?

4. Sometimes we may wonder what difference one person can make. How did Esther change history? (See pages 111–112.) Do you suppose she had any idea of the difference she would make? Give some other examples of people who made a difference in human history.

5. What are the titles given the often weak, fallen church in 1 Peter 2:9?

REFLECT

1. Few churches stand untouched by moral decline. Where have compromises been made? Have churches around you been affected?

2. Put in your own words what C.S. Lewis said about being "far too easily pleased" with what goes on in our churches.

3. The church contributes to individualism and relativism, many times without intention. Name some ways.

4. Why is it vital that the church maintain its distinctiveness from culture?

5. What can you do in your situation to make a difference?

SUMMARIZE

What is the most significant lesson you learned in this study?

APPLY

How will you, as a member of the church, the "royal priesthood," seek to serve the Lord without compromise?

PRAY

Pray that the Lord might give you a vision for what you can do in your church. Pray that he might help you to make a difference in dealing with the loss of character in our congregations.

FURTHER STUDY

Martyn Lloyd-Jones, *Revival*, Crossway Books, 1987.

Leslie Newbigin, *The Household of God*, Friendship Press, 1959.

Charles Swindoll, *Hand Me Another Brick*, Bantam, 1981.

A.W. Tozer, *What Ever Happened to Worship?* Christian Publications, 1985.

Robert Webber & Rodney Clapp, *People of the Truth*, Harper & Row, 1988.

Moral Education

Throughout the history of the church, much emphasis has been placed on the premise that how well we are able to live our Christian lives depends on whether we are able to get and keep a clear conscience. Moral education has been a high priority.

For the apostle Paul, this was a vital goal for everyday Christian living. Without a "good conscience" you can't keep the faith, fight the good fight, or love from a pure heart, Paul wrote to Timothy. Without a good conscience you can't, Paul knew, live a Christian life (1 Timothy 1:5).

Today, as Margaret Thatcher declared to the Church of Scotland, "There is little hope for democracy if the hearts of men and women in democratic societies cannot be touched by a call to something greater than themselves." It's up to people of good conscience to restore this "moral impulse," as Mrs. Thatcher put it, to a nation driven by selfish impulses down a road of corruption and decline. It's our job to re-awaken those internal restraints on selfish preferences that are the substance of character—courage, compassion, duty, and so forth—on which government depends, but cannot create.

READ

Against the Night, chapters 12 and 13
1 Corinthians 8:7–13
1 Corinthians 10:25–30
Titus 1:15–16
1 Timothy 4:1–2

STUDY

1. How have Christians put undue hopes in political processes to bring moral reform? (See pages 115–118.)

2. What did Samuel Johnson say about the limits of government? What did he mean? (See page 118.)

3. Describe the "moral impulse." (See pages 120–123.) How is it related to faith? Who is equipped to quicken it in sleeping consciences? Who is not?

4. Moral virtue is the most essential element of a just society. But once squandered, can it be restored? If not, what then?

5. Robert Bellah refers to the family and church as "communities of memory" because through them are passed the traditions, history, and discipline which provide a context for understanding the world. (See page 127.) How does this happen?

6. Just because we're part of the church does not mean we have a good conscience. Our consciences can be distorted, we see in Titus 1:15–16 and 1 Timothy 4:1–2. Where does this distortion come from?

7. What phrases in 1 Corinthians 8:7–13 and 1 Corinthians 10:25–30 indicate that our consciences need to be educated?

REFLECT

1. Reflect on where you received your moral education. What do you see that bears out Robert Bellah's statement on "communities of memory"?

2. How can parents carry out the task of educating their children's consciences?

3. What, specifically, should the church do to encourage moral education both at home and in church settings?

4. How do we correct our consciences when they are in error? How do we tell if they're in error?

5. Why is it we so often know something to be true—yet refuse to act on it?

6. How can moral education avoid becoming legalistic?

SUMMARIZE

What is the most significant lesson you learned in this study?

APPLY

How will you contribute to the moral education of the next generation?

PRAY

Pray that you might grow in the knowledge and wisdom of God. Pray that you might make a difference in your family or church in encouraging moral education.

FURTHER STUDY

Russell Kirk, *The Wise Men Know What Wicked Things Are Written in the Sky,* Regnery Gateway, Inc., 1987.

Richard Lovelace, *Dynamics of Spiritual Life*, InterVarsity Press, 1979.
John Murray, *Principles of Conduct*, Eerdmanns, 1957.
Francis Schaeffer, *True Spirituality*, Tyndale, 1972.
John Stott, *Involvement*, Vols. 1 & 2, Revell, 1985.

The Church and Repentance

For moral education to take place, the church must *be* the church. It must live up to its task as the body of Christ, the people of God, the creation of the Spirit, a holy nation, a royal priesthood—the locus of spiritual authority.

But first it must repent. Although many believers neglect repentance, the restoration and spiritual vitality of the church demands that it be a repentant community. Though repentance is an unpopular message, because we don't like to confront our sin, repentance is necessary. Francis Schaeffer maintained that Christianity is both the easiest and the hardest religion: easiest because all you have to do is say, "God be merciful to me, a sinner," and hardest because this humbling of ourselves is the very hardest thing to do.

READ

Against the Night, chapters 14 and 15
Psalm 51
Romans 12:2

STUDY

1. Despite the weakness of the church, it is the only institution with the capability to challenge our culture. Why? How are God's transcendent standards of absolute justice and righteousness, the absolute standard of Scripture, and the work of the Holy Spirit all part of the challenge?

2. What does it mean for the "church to be the church"? (See pages 135–136.)

3. What does *metanoia* mean? (See page 140.) How does it change our perspective?

4. What is the first of Martin Luther's 95 Theses? (See page 140.) What does the process of repentance involve, and why is it not a once-in-a-lifetime event?

5. What is striking to you about the story of Cardinal Sin?

6. What phrases in Psalm 51 and the thought of Romans 12:2 stand out to you?

REFLECT

1. Why is it so difficult for us to admit our sin?

2. Why does the renewal of our individual lives or of the church require repentance?

3. Name some attributes of God that, if we pause to consider them, will cause and encourage repentance.

4. What impact could a repentant church have? Why?

SUMMARIZE

What is the most significant lesson you learned from this study?

APPLY

Is yours a life of repentance? What changes in your life-style must you make to maintain a pure, repentant heart?

FURTHER STUDY

G.C. Berkouwer, *Sin*, Eerdmanns, 1971.
J.G. Machen, *The Christian View of Man*, Macmillan, 1939.
Keith Miller, *Overcoming Sin, the Ultimate Addiction*, Harper & Row, 1987.
Bernard Ramm, *Offense to Reason: The Theology of Sin*, Harper & Row, 1985.

Truth and Light

Winston Churchill once said, "Truth is incontrovertible. Panic may resent it; ignorance may deride it; malice may distort it; but there it is." And B. B. Warfield wrote: "We must not, as Christians, assume an attitude of antagonism toward the truths of reason, or the truths of philosophy, or to the truths of science, or to the truths of history, or the truths of criticism. As children of light, we must be careful to keep ourselves open to every ray of light. The church has nothing to fear from truth; but she has everything to fear, and she has already suffered nearly everything, from ignorance. All truth belongs to us as followers of Christ, the Truth, so let us at length enter into our inheritance."

We must not only be people who speak the truth in our culture, but people who live according to it. We must take on the whole Word wholeheartedly: understanding Scripture, memorizing it, letting it dwell richly in us, and allowing his lordship through our thoughts and decisions—to dwell in our flesh.

READ

Against the Night, chapters 16 and 17
John 14:6
Matthew 5:14–16

STUDY

1. Orthodoxy is defined as the solid ground of biblical revelation and the historic confession of Christian truth—the place the church must take its stand. Why is orthodoxy particularly needed in today's relativistic culture?

2. Many religions deal in myth but only Christianity rests on historical fact alone, according to Paul Johnson. How does this truth make Christianity both unique and attractive?

3. Although Scripture is our authoritative source, Scripture and tradition have a long and close relationship. Describe that relationship.

4. The church is to be a light reflecting God's righteousness, justice, and mercy. What strikes you about the communities of light in Zambia, Latin America, Lorton, and Cuba? (See pages 157–161.) Why is it that communities of light often are found in the most difficult situations?

5. What encouraging implications does Matthew 5:14–16 have on the way we face difficult, even painful, challenges to our faith? How is it that, the darker our situation, the better we (and others) are able to see truth?

6. What is our responsibility in the world, according to Matthew 5:14–16?

REFLECT

1. Why do you think Christ is the truth?

---

2. What are the best reasons you know to believe that the Scriptures are true and reliable?

3. We never know until we're there, but how prepared do you feel to be God's representative of truth and light in a situation of total darkness?

SUMMARIZE

What is the most significant lesson you learned from this study?

APPLY

How will you make sure you are walking with a sure step on the path of truth?

PRAY

Pray that you might more clearly know what you believe and why you believe it. Pray that you might be light in a dark world.

FURTHER STUDY

Donald Bloesch, *Crumbling Foundations*, Zondervan, 1984.
F.F. Bruce, *New Testament Documents: Are They Reliable?*, Eerdmanns, 1959.
Josh McDowell, *Evidence that Demands a Verdict*, Vols. 1 & 2, Campus Crusade for Christ, 1979.
R.C. Sproul, *Reasons to Believe*, Zondervan, 1982.

Moral Imagination

Ideas, not laws, bind societies together. As Napoleon declared, "imagination rules the world."

To make an impact on our culture, we must think, and think not only clearly but also creatively from a biblical perspective about all areas of our lives. We must communicate truth in our communities, our families, and churches. Not with a cold, dry exposition of moral principles, however; we must kindle flames.

What we need is a recovery of "moral imagination," a vision of the true and good that can captivate the soul, stir the embers in the heart, and light the imagination. We need a picture of truth that will draw us to the noble task of doing right.

What might this vision and picture be? Moral imagination begins with awe; it sets its eye on the ideal. A vision of moral imagination would include a sense of shared destiny and shared values; a strong, balanced view of the dignity of human life; and a respect for traditions and history.

By appealing to the moral imagination, men and women can touch the hearts and minds of others. It's on this level that the battle for the soul of culture will be ultimately won or lost.

READ

Against the Night, chapters 18 and 19
John 8:31–32
Romans 6:17

STUDY

1. The problem the church faces, according to Charles Malik, "is not only to win souls but to save minds." In presenting the truth, what is inadequate about just quoting Bible verses?

2. Name some ways biblical truth can be presented but neither take the form of Scripture nor betray it. How did Chuck Colson present the principle of restitution as public policy to state legislators? (See page 168.)

3. What is the "moral imagination" to which Colson refers? (See pages 172–173.)

4. Who are some examples of people, or movements throughout history, that sparked the moral imagination? Trace the ways their vision took hold and became reality.

5. What is the relationship between truth and freedom in John 8:31–32?

6. Why is there such a wholehearted obedience in Romans 6:1?

REFLECT

1. Who are the writers or artists who have affected you the most deeply? Why?

2. How can one appeal to the imagination without sacrificing truth to myth or metaphor?

3. Why should we pursue what Harry Blamires calls a "Christian mind"? (See Matthew 22:37 for a start.)

4. What will the development of a "Christian mind" involve for you and your church?

SUMMARIZE

What is the most significant lesson you have learned from this study?

APPLY

How will you change your reading habits and whatever else so that you grow not merely in self-improvement or self-analysis or self-indulgence, but so you can help transform our culture by making the Christian world view appealing to those within your influence?

PRAY

Pray that you will gain the wisdom and discernment to "think Christianly" in every part of your life and schedule. Pray that you would discern fresh ways to communicate truth to your skeptical friends and neighbors.

FURTHER STUDY

Harry Blamires, *The Christian Mind*, Servant Books, 1978.
C.S. Lewis, *Mere Christianity*, Macmillan, 1952.

Against the Night

We have covered much ground in the past studies. We have talked about the problems of individualism and relativism in our culture. We have thought about how the new barbarianism has affected the family, education, government, and the church. We have seen solutions in sparking the moral impulse, restoring a faithful church, recovering a Christian mind, and stimulating the moral imagination. Yet, what difference is this going to make in your life or in the culture?

READ

Against the Night, chapter 20 and review past studies
Psalm 85
Matthew 7:24–27

STUDY

1. Will we succeed in our venture? Does it matter?

2. What have been the most significant new insights you have gained from this book?

3. Which single area do you feel most concerned to act upon?

4. Which institution's decline most concerns you?

5. How much can we do? How much does God do? (See Psalm 85.)

6. What is the rock in Jesus' story of the two builders in Matthew 7:24–27? How are hearing and doing connected?

REFLECT

1. What difference can you, as an individual, make?

2. What difference can your church or study group make?

3. What are some further books that you want to read?

4. What has become the concern of your prayers?

SUMMARIZE

What is the most significant lesson you learned from this study?

APPLY

What is the first thing you will do after finishing this study? Will your life really look or be any different as a result of this study?

PRAY

Pray that God will revive the church and the nation. Use Psalm 85 as the framework for your prayers.

FURTHER STUDY

Charles Colson, *Loving God*, Zondervan, 1983.

Carl F. Henry, *Twilight of a Great Civilization*, Crossway Books, 1988.

James Hitchcock, *What Is Secular Humanism?* Servant Books, 1982.

Russell Kirk, *Roots of American Order*, Open Court, 1974.

Malcolm Muggeridge, *The End of Christendom*, Eerdmans, 1977.

Herbert Schlossberg, *Idols for Destruction*, Nelson, 1983.

Alexander Solzhenitsyn, *A World Split Apart*, Harper & Row, 1978.

George Will, *Statecraft as Soulcraft*, Simon & Schuster, 1983.